THE ANIMALS OF ASIA

BENGAL TIGERS

WILLOW CLARK

PowerKiDS press™

New York

Published in 2013 by The Rosen Publishing Group, Inc.
29 East 21st Street, New York, NY 10010

First Edition

Editor: Joanne Randolph
Book Design: Ashley Drago
Layout Design: Julio Gil

Photo Credits: Cover © PureStock/Age Fotostock; pp. 4, 5, 7, 10, 12–13, 16, 19 (main, inset), 22 Shutterstock.com; p. 8 Comstock Images/Thinkstock; p. 9 (main) iStockphoto/Thinkstock; p. 9 (inset) © www.iStockPhoto.com/Aditya Singh; p. 11 Andy Rouse/The Image Bank/Getty Images; p. 14 © www.iStockphoto.com/Dumrong Khajaroen; p. 15 (main) Tom Brakefield/Stockbyte/Thinkstock; p. 15 (inset) © www.iStockphoto.com/Dawn Nichols; p. 17 Anup Shah/The Image Bank/Getty Images; p. 18 Satyendra Kumar Tiwari/Oxford Scientific/Getty Images; p. 20 Frank Schneidermeyer/Oxford Scientific/Getty Images; p. 21 Joseph Van Os/Oxford Scientific/Getty Images.
Interactive eBook Only: pp. 4, 11, 20 Shutterstock.com; p. 8 Tom Brakefield/Stockbyte/Thinkstock; pp. 12, 17, 18 Fluorescent Films Ltd/Image Bank Film/Getty Images; p. 14 Jupiterimages/Photos.com/Thinkstock.

Library of Congress Cataloging-in-Publication Data

Clark, Willow.
Bengal tigers / by Willow Clark. — 1st ed.
p. cm. — (The animals of Asia)
Includes index.
ISBN 978-1-4488-7417-0 (library binding) — ISBN 978-1-4488-7490-3 (pbk.) —
 ISBN 978-1-4488-7564-1 (6-pack)
1. Bengal tiger—Juvenile literature. I. Title.
QL737.C23C5323 2013
599.756—dc23

                                            2012004239

Manufactured in China

CPSIA Compliance Information: Batch #WKTS12PK: For Further Information contact Rosen Publishing, New York, New York at 1-800-237-9932

CONTENTS

HELLO, TIGER!

Tigers are the largest of the big cats. They are fearsome hunters that are known for their boldly striped coats and roars that can be heard as far as 2 miles (3 km) away. There are eight subspecies, or kinds of tigers, five of which are living today. The subspecies are Siberian, Indochinese, South China, Sumatran, and Bengal tigers.

◄ Tigers have strong, sharp teeth. Their canines, which can be 4 inches (10 cm) long, are the longest of any cat species.

▲
Tigers are huge cats. Their bodies grow to be up to 6 feet (2 m) long, and their tails add another 3 feet (1 m).

Bengal tigers are the most plentiful tiger on Earth. Even so, they are an **endangered species**. This book will tell you more about these Asian animals, their habitat, and the reasons their numbers are falling.

WHERE IN THE WORLD?

The Bengal tiger is found mostly in India. There are smaller populations living in the countries of Bangladesh, Bhutan, China, Myanmar, and Nepal. Bengal tigers like to live in places where there is water for them to drink and plenty of animals for

This map shows where most of the world's Bengal tigers live. ▼

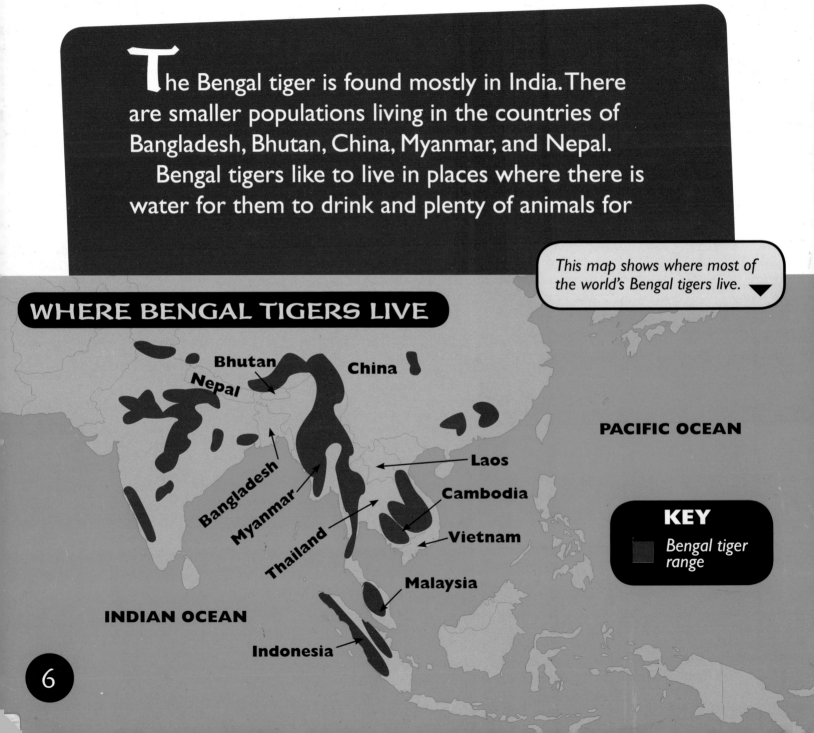

WHERE BENGAL TIGERS LIVE

Bhutan

China

Nepal

PACIFIC OCEAN

Bangladesh

Myanmar

Laos

Cambodia

Thailand

Vietnam

KEY

Bengal tiger range

Malaysia

INDIAN OCEAN

Indonesia

Tigers live in many different habitats in the countries where they live. This one lives in jungles, or rain forests.

them to hunt. They also like places with trees or tall grasses in which they can hide from **prey**. Adult tigers are mostly **solitary** animals. That means they live alone unless they are looking for a **mate** or are raising cubs. Bengal tigers need a lot of space, and as people have spread into once-wild areas, the animals' natural habitat has shrunk. This is one reason Bengal tigers have become endangered.

7

AT HOME IN THE FOREST

Bengal tigers live in a wide range of habitats. They may live anywhere from grasslands to the foothills of the Himalayas. They also live in different kinds of forests, such as tropical forests, temperate forests, and mangrove forests. A mangrove forest

Bengal tigers may live and hunt in swampy wetlands.

▼

Below: *Bengal tigers are not picky about where they live as long as there is plenty of food to eat there.* Right: *Tigers may live in grasslands, especially ones that border forests.*

is a swampy, saltwater forest found in warm coastal areas. Unlike some members of the cat family, tigers are good swimmers. In fact, they are sometimes seen swimming across rivers or between small islands in mangrove forests. Sometimes they swim just to cool off!

TERRITORIAL TIGERS

Unlike lions, tigers do not live in groups. Each adult has a home range, which it will **defend** from other tigers of the same **gender**. Bengal tigers that live where there is lots of prey generally have

If male tigers come across each other in the wild, they are likely to fight. They do not want other males nearby since they could take away food or mates.

smaller ranges than tigers that live where there is less prey.

Tigers communicate with each other by making noises such as roars, grunts, mews, and hisses. Each sound a tiger makes tells other tigers about its mood and where it is. Tigers also communicate with each other by leaving scent markings on their territories. Scent markings act like fences to tell other tigers to keep out!

◀ *This female Bengal tiger is checking for a scent mark. A scent mark tells her another tiger is in the area.*

WHY STRIPES?

The tiger's striped fur certainly makes it memorable, but did you know that it works to **camouflage** the animal? Its coloring of brownish-orange fur with black stripes helps it blend in among tall grasses or in forests. The stripes break up the animal's outline, which helps it further disappear into its surroundings. That means that unsuspecting prey will not see the tiger until it is too late!

Tigers move quietly and count on their striped markings to hide them as they sneak up on prey. ▶

Each tiger has its very own stripe pattern. Although most tigers are brownish orange with black stripes, there are some Bengal tigers that are white with dark stripes.

CLAWS AND JAWS

The Bengal tiger's claws and jaws are two great weapons that help it hunt. Like house cats, tigers have **retractable** claws. That means that their claws can go back into their paws when they are not needed to grab on to prey. This helps keep the tiger's claws sharp. Tigers can also sharpen their claws by scratching trees.

Tigers have four claws that are up to 4 inches (10 cm) long. They have a fifth claw called a dewclaw at the back of each foot. Their dewclaws help them hold on to prey.

This is another way for a tiger to mark its territory.

The tiger's strong jaws have big, sharp **canines**. When hunting smaller prey, Bengal tigers will use their jaws to bite through the animals' neck bones. When hunting larger prey, tigers use their jaws to attack the animals' throats.

Left: *Tigers have muscles in their jaws that let them quickly close their jaws on prey with a huge amount of force.* Bottom: *Tigers have thick pads on the bottoms of their paws. These pads let them move without making any noise as they sneak up on prey.*

ON THE HUNT

Bengal tigers are **carnivores**, or meat eaters, that hunt alone. Between dusk and dawn, they silently stalk prey through their territories. When they get within about 30 feet (9 m) of their prey, they pounce. They grab the animals with their claws,

Tigers count mainly on their sense of sight and hearing to hunt. They try to get as close to their prey as possible before they pounce. ▼

Tigers eat about 88 pounds (40 kg) of meat at a feeding.

pull them to the ground, and kill them with bites to the neck or the throat. After a tiger kills its prey, it drags it to a safe spot and eats.

The hunt is not always successful. Tigers generally make a kill once every 10 to 20 hunts, or about once a week.

ON THE MENU

The tiger is at the top of its **food chain**. It is not on other animals' menus, although lots of animals are on its menu. The Bengal tiger's favorite prey includes wild boar, deerlike animals such as sambar and chital, and cowlike animals such as water buffalo and gaur.

Bengal tigers eat about 50 deer or other animals each year. ▼

Gaurs are relatives to cows and yaks. These huge animals can weigh up to 2,200 pounds (1,000 kg). This means a tiger can eat for a few days if it kills a gaur.

The chital is one of the animals that Bengal tigers like to eat. These deer live in groups of up to 50 animals.

Because hunting is hard work, tigers save the leftovers from their bigger kills. They bury this food in dirt and return to snack on it until it is gone. Tigers are not wasteful. They use their rough, sandpapery tongues to lick every last bit of meat from the animals' bones.

BABY TIGERS

Male and female tigers meet up to mate and then return to their own ranges. Two or three cubs are born three and a half months later. Tigers can mate at any time of year, but it mostly happens between November and April.

Female tigers take care of their babies on their own. They make sure their babies stay safe until they are ready to live on their own. ▼

▲
Newborn tigers do not have good eyesight for many weeks. The tiger's life span is about 8 to 15 years in the wild.

When they are born, Bengal tiger cubs are helpless. The mother must leave them alone in a safe place while she hunts, though. The cubs **nurse** until they are about six months old. Then the mother starts to teach her cubs how to hunt and kill prey. When they are about two years old, the cubs are ready to go off and find their own territories. Female cubs may choose a territory near their mother's territory.

TIGERS IN TROUBLE

There are only about 1,850 Bengal tigers left in the wild. These animals are in trouble due to habitat loss as well as **poaching.** Growing human populations are pushing tigers out of their natural habitat. People may also illegally kill tigers for their skin or to protect their livestock.

Groups like the World Wildlife Fund are working to raise awareness about endangered animals like Bengal tigers. They also encourage countries to make and enforce laws that protect animals and their habitats. Their goal is to make sure that Bengal tigers' numbers grow so that they do not become **extinct**.

▲
The number of tigers in the wild has dropped by more than 50 percent in the past 10 years and continues to go down.

GLOSSARY

CAMOUFLAGE (KA-muh-flahj) To hide by looking like the things around one.

CANINES (KAY-nynz) Pointy teeth found on the side of the mouth, in front.

CARNIVORES (KAHR-neh-vorz) Animals that eat only other animals.

DEFEND (dih-FEND) To guard from harm.

ENDANGERED (in-DAYN-jerd) In danger of no longer living.

EXTINCT (ik-STINGKT) No longer existing.

FOOD CHAIN (FOOD CHAYN) A group of living things that are each other's food.

GENDER (JEN-der) Relating to an animal's sex, male or female.

MATE (MAYT) A partner for making babies.

NURSE (NURS) When a female feeds her baby milk from her body.

POACHING (POHCH-ing) Hunting animals when it is against the law.

PREY (PRAY) An animal that is hunted by another animal for food.

RETRACTABLE (rih-TRAK-tuh-bel) Able to be pulled back.

SOLITARY (SAH-leh-ter-ee) Liking to be alone.

SPECIES (SPEE-sheez) One kind of living thing. All people are one species.

INDEX

WEBSITES

Due to the changing nature of Internet links, PowerKids Press has developed an online list of websites related to the subject of this book. This site is updated regularly. Please use this link to access the list: www.powerkidslinks.com/aoa/beng/